Photo Album of the Greek Resistance

Costa G. Couvaras

PHOTO ALBUM
of the
GREEK RESISTANCE

Preface by L. S. Stavrianos

Wire Press - San Francisco
1978

Cover and book design by Dino Siotis

ISBN 0-918034-02-7
Library of Congress catalog card number 78-65147

Wire Press, 392 San Jose Avenue, San Francisco, Ca 94110

Contents

Preface

The subject of this book is the second Greek War of Independence -- the war waged by the National Liberation Front (EAM) and its National Popular Liberation Army (ELAS). But whereas the first War of Independence was successful and Greece became politically independent, the second War of Independence was unsuccessful and Greece has remained economically dependent.

After every war it is the victors who write its history. If the first War of Independence had failed, the Philike Hetairia would have been written off as an organization of traitors and/or fools, as indeed it was condemned at the time by the Turks and their Greek puppets. Since the second War of Independence failed (for external rather than internal reasons), the victors turned fact into myth, and myth into fact. The EAM-ELAS, which was the heart and soul of the resistance, became an antinational conspiracy of communism and pan-Slavism. Churchill and Truman and their puppet politicians and scribes in Greece brainwashed an entire generation just as thoroughly as Hitler and Goebbels brainwashed an entire generation in Germany.

Those who attempted to resist the brainwashing paid dearly for their efforts, as illustrated by the fate of leaders such as Stefanos Sarafis amd Grigoris Lambrakis. What happened to them is well-known, but what is not known is the persecution of Greek-Americans who attempted to resist the brainwashing in the United States. The story of this small group of patriots is important for American history as well as Greek. It is a story that has not been told, and that should be told.

7

One of the leaders of this group is Costa Couvaras. He suffered persecution by the FBI and CIA when he returned to the United States and attempted to inform the American people of what was really going on in Greece. But he persisted, and has made important contributions in setting the record straight. In 1976 he published "O.S.S. ME TIN KENTRIKI TOU EAM" (Exantas). With the present collection of photographs taken during his O.S.S. mission to occupied Greece, we get some of the flavor and spirit of the EAM-ELAS movement, which for so long has been so shamefully traduced.

We are all intebted to Costa Couvaras for this contribution, which is as enjoyable as it is significant. And we look forward to more works based on his unique experiences and observations in occupied Greece.

L. S. Stavrianos
Emeritus Professor of History, Northwestern University.
Adjunct Professor of History, University of California, San Diego.

Prologue

A glorious page in the long history of Greece was written by the resistance movement of the country during the German and Italian occupation in World War II. However, to this day the achievements of the Greek guerrillas have remained, to a great extent, unappreciated. The reason for this phenomenon is that the country had been divided during the occupation into rightist and leftist factions fighting each other. After liberation, the rightists, many of whom collaborated with the enemy, took over the government though they were in the minority. It was with the help of the British and American allies, and an ensuing civil war, that the rightists managed to control the country for the last thirty five years. The culmination of this control was a juntä that ruled Greece for seven long years, and finally managed to bring the Turkish invasion of the island of Cyprus, with untold suffering on the part of the people and the occupation of 40% of the island by the Turkish army.

This book of photographs is a small contribution to a great period of Greek history, and in a small way wishes to pay tribute to all those who believed they were doing the right thing in fighting the enemy occupiers of their country.

As an American intelligence officer, I was privileged to have worked with the Greek resistance movement and to have seen the Greek guerrillas in action and to have reported that action to the United States government. I was also able to take photographs of the activities of the resistance fighters and their political leadership. It is these photographs that I present to the general public as a historical monument of what happened at that time.

Costa G. Couvaras

Glendale, California, Summer 1978

Entering Occupied Greece

WE ENTER GREECE

In this thirty foot caique we got to Greece from an American base thirty miles north of Smyrna, and across the southern part of the island of Mytilini. Our destination was the small hamlet of Othonia, in the middle section of the island of Evia. It took us eight days to reach our goal. Because of bad weather we had to turn back twice and hide on the Turkish coast across from the island of Chios. Another time we found a hiding place in a deserted cove on the island of Skyros. Finally, through the ability of our captain Manolis, whose last name I don't remember, and his assistant and boat mechanic Vafiades, whose first name escapes me, we entered on a rainy and foggy night, the little bay of Othonia. Our first night in Greece was spent in a stable, in the company of a nice gray donkey. We were so tired, though, that the accommodations did not bother our sleep.

THE GREEK GUERRILLAS EXTEND A WELCOME TO THE PERICLES MISSION

We met our first guerrillas next morning after our arrival at a near-by location called Calamos. Our small group had hiked to Calamos across from the little bay of Othonia before the boat arrived. The guerrillas were happy to welcome us at their hut, and share with us what little food they had. These young men were better dressed and better equipped than the guerrillas we met in later days on our hike to the mountains. Calamos was the place that the British and American missions used to enter and leave Greece, and these guerrillas were the beneficiaries of arms and equipment from the foreigners that would pass by. This picture, in addition to guerrillas, shows a couple of political commissars of the ELAS. Captain Manolis and mechanic Vafiades are standing on the right with 9mm automatis on their shoulders. Between them, looking toward the boat, is Yannis Kakossaios, who had joined the Pericles Mission in Cairo as our liaison with EAM-ELAS.

14

WELL SUPPLIED GUERRILLAS

Five of the guerrillas that welcomed us at the outpost of Calamos. All of them young, and rather well supplied with weapons that were mostly provided by the foreign missions --English and American -- that were passing through this outpost. We also presented these guerrillas with a few automatic weapons.

16

THE OLD AND THE NEW

Two young guerrillas at Calamos in front of the hut where we slept for the first two nights. The one on the left poses with his old regular rifle of World War I vintage. The one on the right is holding an up-to-date automatic weapon.

GUERRILLA POSING

A guerrilla of the Calamos outpost posing with his rifle, bandoliers, and dagger.

"TARZAN" POSES FOR A PICTURE

I had no difficulty getting guerrillas to pose for me, individually or in groups. That was something they all loved to do. However, all of them were very serious people and very idealistic. Becoming guerrillas, they knew they were going to suffer, and their families were going to suffer as well, but they believed in the cause of freedom, and were willing to accept the consequences. Guerrilla life, as I witnessed it, was no bed of roses. In fact, it was a very difficult and exacting sort of existence. The Greek guerrilla suffered many privations. He was always short of food, and whatever food there was to go around was of low quality. Two meals a day was the norm. I never wrote down the names of the people I photographed because my purpose for getting into Greece was not picture taking. This fellow had the name "Tarzan" written on the side of his rifle, and that is the name we had to call him by.

NEW WEAPON — OLD CLOTHES

On the island of Evia this guerrilla poses with a brand new automatic weapon. His clothing was in pretty bad shape. His shoes were falling apart, and his pants were real old. Such minor inconveniences, though, didn't bother these people. What most of them would tell me was: "Give us enough weapons to be able to recruit more men, and we'll chase the Germans out of our country."

THE THIRD BATTALION OF EVIA

At the village of Manikia, we met with the Third Battalion of the island of Evia. The man in the middle of this picture is Prokopis Longos, the Captain of the Battalion, who had been a major in the regular Greek army. He joined the guerrillas, and became head of this unit of approximately 300 men. The dress of the guerrillas, as did their weapons, varied from man to man. The dress was made up of what each man could get his hands on; old army uniforms, Italian uniforms, civilian dress of any kind, and whatever shoes were available. Some guerrillas had no shoes at all. Weapons consisted of some automatics given as gifts by the British or American missions passing through the island. But the majority of the weapons were Greek army rifle of World War I vintage or captured Italian rifles from the Albanian campaign or from the more recent Italian surrender. However, weapons were not plentiful, and some of the guerrillas had none.

RUSSIANS SURRENDER TO THE GUERRILLAS

These are Russian soldiers who performed guard duty for the Germans in occupied countries. They were part of the Russian prisoners of war who had surrendered to the Nazis in the Eastern Front. The day before we reached the Evia Third Battalion, they had surrendered to the guerrillas. The total number was twelve, and they had come with all their weapons, including two machine guns. When we met them they seemed very happy to have surrendered and cut off their connection with the Nazis.

THE DONKEY CARAVAN

This is the start of our trek towards the mountains of central Greece. In this picture we witness the loading of a donkey. At the beginning we had fourteen such loads. Soon we found out, however, that we were carrying too much, and we had to leave a great deal of our things behind, hoping to be able to retrieve them at a later day. In occupied Greece it was not easy to find animals to move you from one place to another. Besides, danger always lurked nearby. The bigger the caravan, the bigger the target it would make, and the more people would talk about it in the places we passed. The tall young man on the left in this picture is Constantine Papadopoulos, who was the radio operator of the Pericles Mission. He came from Newark, New Jersey, and at the time was a non-commissioned officer of the U.S. Navy. In the Greek mountains he was known as "Alex."

Starting the Trek Towards the Mountains

PAVLOS — THE FIRST GUERRILLA ESCORT OF THE PERICLES MISSION

Pavlos had joined the Pericles Mission somewhere in central Greece, and became our guard and companion on our trek toward EAM headquarters, and as long as we stayed in the town of Carpenissi. Pavlos was one of the first guerrillas, having joined Aris Velouhiots' band at the age of 18. He was able to tell me a great deal about Aris and early guerrilla life and activities. Pavlos was never told that he was working for an American secret mission. At one time, though, he confided in me that his ambition was, after the war, to go to America and open a restaurant!

BURNED TOWN OF CARPENISSI

       This is the section of the town of Carpenissi as we found it in the middle of May, 1944. The Germans had gotten there some time before our arrival and had destroyed part of that town. The Carpenissi high school had been burned down, as well as the main hotel and some of the neighborhoods. However, some parts of the town were left intact, and we were able to get a nice house for ourselves. Eventually, in another attack, the rest of the town was destroyed.

NIKOS ZAIMIS JOINED THE GUERRILLAS UNDER PRESSURE

This man did not join the guerrillas because he believed in ideals. He became an outlaw originally because he had killed a man in his village for family reasons. Eventually, the guerrillas persuaded him to join the struggle and fight the enemies of his country. He became part of our group, hiking towards the mountains of central Greece to EAM headquarters and he professed to believe in the ideals the EAM was fighting for.

MOUNTAIN LANDSCAPE

This picture was taken outside a guerrilla lookout in the mountains of central Greece. The man on the right is Yannis Kakosaios, the liaison of the Pericles Mission with the resistance movement, who had accompanied us from Cairo.

DAILY BREAD

These are children of the town of Carpenissi, waiting to get their daily meal from the EAM soup kitchen that was organized with food provided by the International Red Cross. These food kitchens were organized towards the end of the war in the liberated parts of Greece after a great fight, because the Germans were reluctant in permitting Red Cross food to enter regions controlled by the guerrillas. In places where there was no distribution of food, children were starving, and their bodies were full of sores, an indication of lack of necessary nutrients.

ENEMY SPIES!

　　These five children, aged 8 to 12, were caught by the local organization of Mount Peleon as German spies! Some German intelligence officer in the city of Volos noticed them looking for food in the garbage cans of this army unit, offered them some food and promised more if they would go to the village around the city to find out where ELAS guerrillas were concentrated. The Village Resistance Organization spotted them, caught them, and not knowing what to do with them, sent them to Headquarters. When I found out about them, they ate and slept in prison, but in the daytime they were free to roam the town of Carpenissi.

GERMAN PRISONERS OF THE GUERRILLAS

At the end of the summer, 1944, I visited a German prisoner of war camp that ELAS guerrillas had organized near a village in the center of the Pindos mountain range. The situation of the prisoners was not by any stretch of the imagination idealistic, although the landscape surrounding the camp was beautiful. However, these prisoners should have been happy to be alive. Before this period, which coincided with the end of the war, neither the Germans, nor the guerrillas kept any prisoners. Both executed their prisoners as soon as they caught them. In this camp existence was rough, but the prisoners ate two meals a day and were treated humanely. In fact, the guerrilas did not fare any better than the prisoners. In the food line, I noticed a guerrilla dishing out food to a prisoner wearing only underdrawers. When I questioned him, he said he had no pants (there was a strict order not to take anything from the prisoners). He was lucky, though. Next day I sent him a pair of nice American army pants from a parachute drop we received a few days before.

PRISONER OF WAR CAMP COMMANDER

As much as I have tried, I have not been able to remember this man's name, although we had many discussions together after we reached the guerrilla headquarters. What I remember about him is that he was an old communist from Athens and was trusted by the leadership. That is probably the reason that he was appointed head of the camp of German prisoners. In this picture he is wearing the "black hat" (Mavroskoufis) an honor usually reserved for the entourage of the guerrilla leader, Aris Velouhiotis.

WOMEN IN THE RESISTANCE MOVEMENT

Women played a great part in the Greek resistance movement. They will always be remembered as great fighters and heads of local organizations. They also contributed as carriers of provisions and equipment to the fighting units in forward positions, carrying everything on their backs or on the backs of their pack animals.

WITH RIFLE AND A CROSS FIGHTING THE ENEMY

"Papa" Holevas, a priest of Central Greece, joined the guerrillas to fight for liberation and social justice. He was not unique. Other priests all over the country had joined the guerrilla movement. The higher clergy of Greece were also represented in EAM-ELAS headquarters. The Bishop of Kozani was a regular at headquarters, and played an important role in an advisory capacity. Both he and the Bishop of Pyrgos participated in the deliberations of the "National Assembly" that took place in the village of Korishades in early June, 1944. A picture that has stayed in my mind all these years is of the Bishop of Pyrgos taking the oath at the podium of the Assembly as I was entering the hall.

INTELLECTUALS IN THE GREEK RESISTANCE

Many Greek intellectuals joined the resistance movement, basically in the cities, where they used their talents as editors of underground newspapers and as authors of anti-enemy tracts. They performed the same functions in the mountains with the guerrillas. In this picture Vassilis Rotas, a well known writer and theatrical producer from Athens, talks with the priest of the village of Klistos and two guerrillas.

THIS UNIFORM HAD SEEN BETTER DAYS

      I met this man one day during my hikes to the villages of the central Agrafa region. What attracted me and made me take his picture was his peculiar uniform, which was not the regular one of the average guerrilla, but the uniform of the former royal guard. He was a guerrila and from the way he carried his rifle one could see that he had good army training. In talking to him, I found out he had been with the royal guard in the past, and when he joined the guerrillas he found nothing better to wear than his old uniform. The rest of his dress was makeshift. An old hand woven sweater, old village stockings, and old army shoes.

Women Guerrillas

MEN AND WOMEN GUERRILLAS TRAINING TOGETHER

A mixed group of men and women guerrillas, part of the 13th Guerrilla Brigade of Central Greece, training together at the town of Carpenissi in June 1944. The women guerrillas were new and the men, as veterans of a number of campaigns, were showing them how to use the various weapons.

HE TRAINED THE WOMEN

This young officer of the regular army of Greece was appointed to train the women's group in the use of arms that included rifles, automatic weapons and machine guns. The woman on the left is Georgia Callidou who now lives in Athens and is married to a former guerrilla leader.

THREE FEMALE FIGHTERS

These three women guerrillas are full of enthusiasm and ready to fight the enemies of their country. The woman in the middle is Thyela, a veteran of many encounters with the enemy, who claimed the title of the first woman guerrilla of Greece.

THYELA BECAME THE FIRST WOMAN GUERRILLA

This is Thyela (Tempest), who claimed to be the first woman guerrilla of Greece. When I met her in Spring of 1944, she was a veteran of many battles against the Germans and against rival guerrilla bands. In this picture she is wearing a pair of blue pants, which was against regulations, but she had earned this right for capturing a colonel, whom she forced to exchange his blue trousers for her own skirt. Thyela believed strongly in the struggle at hand. She was full of idealism and determination in the fight against fascism, and in the struggle against what she considered the internal enemies of the working class. After liberation, she went to Athens to be near her small daughters, and took part in the December, 1944, civil war. There she was killed by British fire near the National Theatre in the center of Athens. Her real name was Meni Papaliou. She had been married to a police officer whom she left to join the guerrillas. Thyela was an intelligent woman, who at times carried a sensitive expression on her face. At other times, her face reflected great determination and un-shakable belief for the struggle in which she was participating. She believed strongly that because of the efforts of the resistance movement, a better Greece would emerge. A country "with liberty and justice for all."

FIRST WOMAN GUERRILLA

This is Thyela again. A lovely, but ferocious fighter. In certain instances she put her co-fighters and her enemies to shame with her spirit and her disregard for danger.

TEACHING THEM TO SHOOT

Women guerrillas learn the art of shooting light weapons from an expert, a former regular army officer.

The "Pericles" Group

THE PERICLES MISSION

Left to right, "Uncle Costas" Lykouris, general assistant to the head of the Pericles Mission, me and Iacovos Yacoumis, guard to the mission. In rear, Constantine Papadopoulos, U.S. Navy non-commissioned officer, radio operator of the Pericles Mission.

PERICLES' CHIEF

A photo of myself taken when I was the head of the Pericles Mission. My rank was First Lieutenant, U.S. Army Intelligence.

GENERAL ASSISTANT TO PERICLES MISSION

Costas Lycouris, a former furniture polisher from Athens, became a communist early in life and spent many years in prison during the oppressive Metaxas dictatorship. "Uncle Costas" was an excellent assistant to me in the mountains. He was dependable and extremely efficient. He copied documents by hand better than could be done by typewriter and without errors. After liberation he spent many years in concentration camps and island exile.

GATHERING PARACHUTES

In August, 1944, a parachute drop was made to the Pericles Mission which personally gave me a great deal of trouble. In the first place, the plane came to our *rendezvous* two hours early one night and we were afraid to light the signal fires lest it be an enemy plane. Altogether, we had to stay on a mountain top for eighteen days, waiting for the plane to return. When it finally came, the parachutes fell inside ravines and on mountain tops, far from our waiting place. Meanwhile, rain and cold had made our lives miserable. However, we were happy to receive the supplies which consisted of clothes, money, our mail, books and cigarettes for the mission, plus a small number of arms. The photo shows the gathering place of the parachutes with me on the left. Our two Italian prisoners prisoners of war in the middle and my guerrilla guard on the right.

THE BATTLE OF HARVEST

During the summer of 1944 it was feared that the Germans would take away the harvest of the Thessaly Plain. The guerrillas organized groups to help the farmers gather and store the harvest so that the enemy could not lay hands on it. The photo shows a threshing floor where the horses threshed the wheat in a hurry.

82

ITALIAN PRISONERS OF THE GUERRILLAS ASSIST US

In our vigil on the mountain, two Italian prisoners, Giussepe and Lazzaro, joined our group. They were dressed in rags with no shoes and had very little food. We fed them well while they were with us and they reciprocated by singing beautiful Italian songs at our nightly gatherings around the fire. After the drop we gave them cans of food and new clothes to wear.

EAM Guerrilla Leadership

YANNIS IOANNIDES

He was the second secretary of the Greek Communist Party and while I was in the mountains, the one designated to deal with intelligence matters. That means the man with whom I had to deal directly for my work. He was very smart and I had no difficulty in making him understand my point of view. I can say that in my dealings with him no difficulties of any kind arose.

AN EXCURSION WITH THE COMMUNIST LEADERSHIP

Yannis Ioannides and his wife, Domna, among other leaders of the Communist Party of Greece, on an excursion to a peak of the Pindos Range. At the far right, standing, Yannis Zevgos, communist intellectual and historian, who became Minister of Agriculture in the Unity Government that was formed after liberation.

LEADER OF THE COMMUNISTS

Yorghos Siantos, First Secretary of the Communist Party of Greece, traveling, in a motor boat towards Athens as German troops were leaving the city. At the left Costas Gavrielides, leader at the time of the Agrarian Party of Greece.

GREEK ARMY GENERAL WITH RUSSIAN OFFICER

General Emanuel Mantakas of the regular Greek Army, who had joined the guerrillas, talks with Colonel Popoff, head of the Russian Mission to the Greek guerrillas. This photo was taken going through the Gulf of Corinth during a motor boat trip to Athens.

INTELLECTUALS WITH THE GUERRILLAS

A group of intellectuals, authors, newspapermen and artists, returning to Athens in a motor boat that carried the Communist leadership. In middle rear, a Russian officer, member of the Mission to ELAS.

RUSSIAN HEAD OF MISSION

Colonel Popoff, head of the Russian mission to ELAS guerrillas, traveling to Athens in a motor boat with Greek Communist Party leadership.

Civil War and Aftermath

EAM PARADE AFTER LIBERATION

Impressive parades by EAM followers took place in Athens during the latter part of October, 1944, and had the effect of scaring the Greek Right with their agressiveness and vigor.

FOREIGN CORRESPONDENTS IN LIBERATED ATHENS

Foreign correspondents, mostly Americans, started coming into Athens soon after liberation. In this picture are two of the better known ones, Leland Stowe, right, and George Weller, both good friends of mine.

ON THE ACROPOLIS

Foreign correspondent George Weller of the Chicago Daily News with me on the Acropolis. Ten years earlier I had worked as a translator for George Weller when the latter was correspondent in Greece for the New.York Times.

CIVIL WAR

The civil war, or the "December Events" as that period is known in Greece, started on December 3, 1944. On that fateful day, before my eyes, about twenty people were killed and many more wounded by the Athens police. This photo shows blood spilled in the street as a result of shooting which lasted about a half hour.

108

BODIES ARE CARRIED TO THE CEMETERY

　　　　Caskets with the bodies of some of the victims of the December 3rd shooting are carried on
a truck to the cemetery the day after the shooting.

110

BRITISH PLANES HIT ATHENS SUBURBS

Houses in an Athens suburb that were destroyed by British bombings during the days following the December 3rd events.

ΔΙΑΒΑΤΗ ΤΟ ΜΟΝΟΠΑΤΙ
ΑΥΤΟ ΟΔΗΓΕΙ ΣΤΟΥΣ ΤΑ
ΦΟΥΣ ΤΩΝ ΗΡΩΩΝ ΠΟΥ ΕΠΕΣΑΝ
ΓΙΑ ΤΗ ΛΕΥΤΕΡΙΑ ΚΑΙ
ΤΗ ΛΑΟΚΡΑΤΙΑ
ΤΗΣ

GRAVE MARKER OF A CITY FIGHTER

Marker on the grave of an EAM fighter which was destroyed by Greek rightists during the December 3rd events.

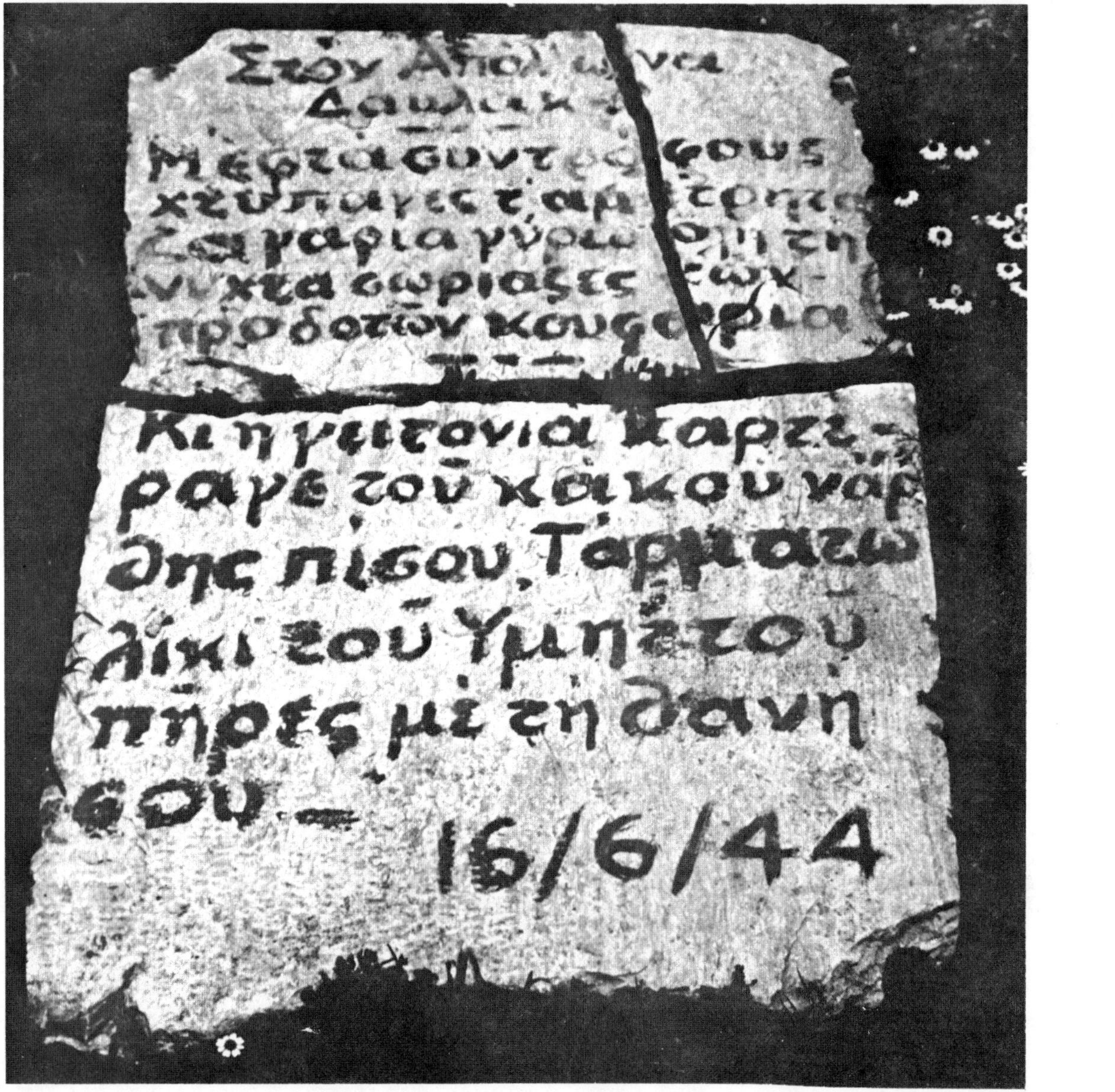
Κι η γειτονια καρτε-
ραγε του κακου ναρ
θης πισου. Ταρματω
λικι του Υμηττου
πηρες με τη θανη
σου —
16/6/44

GUERRILLAS WITHDRAW TO THESSALY

After the fighting in Athens, the guerrillas withdrew towards the Province of Thessaly and I was commissioned by the OSS to visit his old friends in the EAM movement to determine their intentions for the future. This photograph was taken at a stop in the narrows of ancient Thermopylae.

POST CIVIL WAR DEMONSTRATION

An anti-government and anti-British demonstration that took place in the city of Lamia after the fighting in Athens.

THE WRITING ON THE WALL

"Down with the new chains." By this expression, "new chains", EAM meant British chains, which supposedly came after the German chains.

NICOS CARVOUNIS

Nicos Carvounis, an important Greek intellectual, joined the resistance movement at its very inception. Eventually, he went to the mountains and worked as propaganda chief of the EAM movement and editor in chief of the EAM newspaper, ELEFTHERI ELLADA. He was a relative of mine.

TWO OSS MISSIONS MEET

Two OSS missions met in the city of Trikala at the beginning of February, 1945. Left, U.S. Navy Officer, Chris Kantianis, head of the American Mission at Trikala, welcomes me in the center of the photograph. They are surrounded by a Greek-American family which had been stranded in Greece during the war.

LT. COUVARAS WITH THE HEAD OF THE GREEK GUERRILLAS

I met the head of the Greek guerrillas, Aris Velouhiotis, for the first time in the city of Tri-kala after the defeat of ELAS in the Athens civil war. "Aris," as he was known all over Greece, impressed me as the greatest of the EAM-ELAS leaders whom I had met during my sojourn in Greece.

ARIS VELOUHIOTIS

His real name was Thanassis Claras. He was a man of small stature, but impressive in bearing and speech. He started as a guerrilla fighter with few followers. By the end of the war, he was commanding an army of over 70.000. A few months after we met, in the same city of Trikala, his head was hanging on a telephone pole. He was executed by Greek rightists.

Return to Ithaca

COMMUNICATING WITH THE BASE

A radio telegrapher of the Pericles Mission with his receiver on a jeep and antenna spread around him, trying to contact Cairo from a meadow near the ancient Roman city of Nicopolis in the Province of Epirus.

LOOKING FOR "ITHACA SMOKE TO RISE"

This photo shows me on a motor boat in June, 1945, looking through the morning mist towards my ancestral island of Ithaca to which I was returning after an absence of ten years. During my sojourn in the mountains and while the Germans were still in the country, I did not dare contact my sister, fearing German reprisals against my family if it became known that I was with the Greek guerrillas.

136

RETURN TO ITHACA

Photo of a sailboat in the Ionian Sea taken in the early morning as it was approaching the island of Ithaca. Communication among the islands and between the islands and the mainland was carried on by these small sailboats and motor boats because all steamships had been destroyed during the war.